SHREK™

JOKE BOOK

By Sarah Fisch
and Howie Dewin

SCHOLASTIC

Scholastic Children's Books
Commonwealth House, 1-19 New Oxford Street
London WC1A 1NU, UK
a division of Scholastic Ltd
London ~ New York ~ Toronto ~ Sydney ~ Auckland
Mexico City ~ New Delhi ~ Hong Kong

First published in the USA by Scholastic Inc., 2004
First published in the UK by Scholastic Ltd, 2004

ISBN 0 439 96304 4

Printed and bound by Nørhaven Paperback, Denmark

2 4 6 8 10 9 7 5 3 1

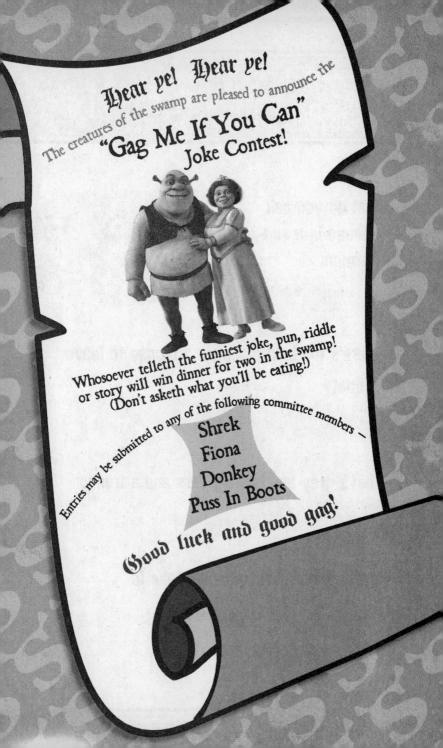

From the Law Offices of the Three Blind Mice

We fight injustice wherever we see it!

What do you call a mouse in a suit of armour?

A no-dent rodent!

Where's the best place for a mouse to leave his boat?

The Hickory Dickory Dock.

What's grey and has big ears and a trunk?

A mouse on vacation.

How many blind mice does it take to change a light bulb?

Oh, come on! Who needs light?

Are You A Blind Mouse?

IF

YOUR

TAIL IS

MISSING

B4UCTHECAT

THEANSWERISYES

We want you to feel at home!

What vegetable do you get when Shrek runs through your garden?

Squash!

Why did Baby Bear cross the playground?

To get to the other slide.

Does Goldilocks get enough to eat when she has dinner with Mama, Papa and Baby?

Bearly.

What do you call Baby Bear's great-grandmother and great-grandfather?

The Three Bears' Forebears.

Goldilocks's Guide to Dining Out . . .

If your eggs move fast,
they're too runny.

If your hamburger won't put
down its book, it's too read.

If your toast asks questions
you can't answer, it's too hard.

If your mother tells you to eat
your greens and you
don't want to, it's too bad.

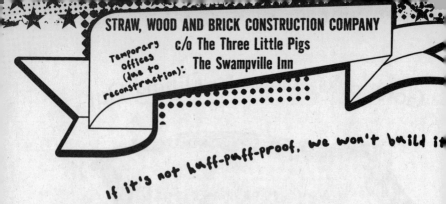

STRAW, WOOD AND BRICK CONSTRUCTION COMPANY
c/o The Three Little Pigs
The Swampville Inn

Temporary offices (due to reconstruction):

If it's not huff-puff-proof, we won't build it

What do you call a pig with three eyes?

A pi-i-ig.

What do you get when you cross a pig with a robot?

A cy-pork!

What do you call it when a pig runs away?

A ham scram!

What do you get when you cross Pinocchio with a pig?

Pine swine!

If a red house is made of red bricks, a blue house is made from blue bricks and a pink house is made from pink bricks – what's a green house made from?

GLASS!

What's the Three Pigs' favourite horror movie?

The Texas Chain-sow Massacre!

What does a pig wear when he gets dressed up?

A pigsty.

What do you use when you arrest a bad pig?

Hamcuffs.

Why do pigs like to spend so much time in the kitchen?

Because we always feel like bacon.

Pinocchio vs Gingerbread Man

Why does Pinocchio like to float in the ocean?

He wants to be a real buoy!

Why does Pinocchio always stop lying when his nose gets to be eleven inches long?

Because he doesn't want it to turn into a foot!

What do you get when you cross Pinocchio with chocolate custard?

Wooden pudding!

What do you get when you cross a DJ with the Gingerbread Man?

Sweet beats.

How many gingerbread men does it take to change a light bulb?

Two — one to change the bulb, and the other to scrape the burnt parts off him.

Why was the Gingerbread Man crying?

Because his mum was a wafer so long.

Glass Slipper inc.

c/o PRINCE CHARMING & CINDERELLA
charming castle, Penthouse
Far Far Away 12000

Let us shatter your notions of footwear.

Why couldn't Prince Charming get down from the tower?

Because he was totally stuck-up.

What do you call Prince Charming after a sword fight with Puss In Boots?

Minced Charming!

How did Shrek feel when he saw Princess Fiona talking to Prince Charming?

He was green with envy!

Why did Cinderella get kicked off the basketball team?

Because she ran away from the ball.

Why was Cinderella such a bad athlete?

Because her coach was a pumpkin!

How many Prince Charmings does it take to change a light bulb?

One. He just holds it in the air and waits for the world to revolve around him!

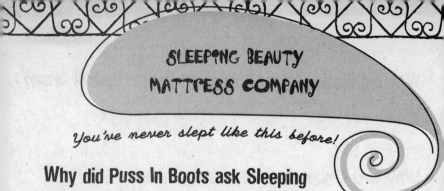

SLEEPING BEAUTY MATTRESS COMPANY

You've never slept like this before!

Why did Puss In Boots ask Sleeping Beauty to help him find new slippers?

He wanted a sleeping bootie.

Why did Sleeping Beauty fall asleep at the camera shop?

She was waiting for her prints to come.

Why weren't the Three Little Pigs invited to the royal ball?

Because they're so boar-ing.

TOP TEN WAYS TO TELL IF YOUR PRINCE IS A FROG:

10 He gets a little too excited when there are flies in the house.

9 He gets jumpy in French restaurants.

8 His best friends live in the pond.

7 It takes a day to get him out of the bath.

6 He thinks he's related to salad, broccoli and anything else that's green.

5 He uses his tongue to do the dusting.

4 He always wins underwater swimming contests.

3 You can't find his toes.

2 Kermit is his favourite actor.

1 There's always a wet mark when he gets off a chair.

What did the frog do when he heard my jokes?

He croaked up.

What do you call Puss In Boots when he steals potions from the Fairy Godmother?

A cat burglar!

How many Fairy Godmothers does it take to change a light bulb?

It depends what you want to change it into. . .

What did the witch request when she stayed at a hotel?

Broom service.

That Spells Trouble!

Frog Spell + Bunny Spell = A Ribbit

Frog Spell + Eye Doctor Spell = Hoptician

Frog Spell + Vegetable Spell = Green Bean

Frog Spell + Hero Spell = Knight in Sliming Armour

Rhyme Time

Create your own spells.
All you need are a couple
of rhymes for some of the
important ingredients and you'll be
making spells in no time! For example:

Newt Eye: Fruit Pie: Mute Guy

Squeeze the juice of a newt eye into a fruit pie
and turn talkers into mute guys.

Frog Gut: Dog Butt: Bog Mutt

One cup of frog gut rubbed on to a dog's butt turns
enemies to bog mutts.

Scum Slime: Some Time: Dumb Crime

Boil some scum slime and stir it for some time, and
your rival will be arrested for doing a dumb crime.

Why do so many rabbits play in Rumpelstiltskin's garden when he spins straw into gold?

They heard he was making carats!

What did Rumpelstiltskin say when the reporter asked if he could call him by his first name?

Be my guess.

What did Rumpelstiltskin say when the young girl finally guessed "Rumpelstiltskin"?

That's my gnome!

Rumpelstiltskin's Top Ten Great Names for a Baby

10. Beetsme
9. Guessagain
8. Idunno
7. Gimmeahint
6. Amiright

5. Imstumped
4. Whoknows
3. Noclue
2. Tizzamystery
1. Youllneverguess

Three Kitten
Misplaced Mitten Store
3 Cantfindit Boulevard
Far Far Away 33333

You choose it,
we lose it.

We make it our business
to operate at a loss.

What happened when the mama cat ate a ball of wool?

She had mittens!

Who do the three little kittens still believe in?

Santa Claws.

What do kittens get after they've been playing out in the forest?

Fir coats.

More than
3,000,000
mittens lost!

What do kittens say when they get a spanking for losing their mittens?

Me-Ow!

Why are kittens so small?

Because we only drink condensed milk.

Who's the funniest of them all?

SHREK!

What happens when Shrek . . .

. . . falls off a boat?

He goes ogreboard.

. . . eats too much?

He gets ogreweight.

. . . burns his dinner?

The food gets ogredone.

. . . gets too emotional?

He is ogrecome.

. . . has buck-teeth?

He's got an ogrebite.

Ode to Green

Green is the colour of
my true love's skin.
It's the sheen on the mould
for penicillin.
It's the colour you will see
if you witness me grin
and the shade of the
bogeys I pull from within.

Top Ten Reasons Shrek Is in a Bad Mood

10. His favourite meals have all just been declared endangered species.

9. He fell in the swamp and got a little bogged down.

8. Fiona cleaned the house.

7. He ran out of his favourite cologne, Mould Spice.

6. It's not easy being green.

5. He was playing chess with Fiona, and he got Shrek-mated.

4. The swamp diner stopped serving his favourite breakfast, toe jam and toast.

3. He's got a bad case of swamp gas.

2. Donkey ate all his favourite ice cream, Bogeys n' Cream.

And the number one reason Shrek is having a bad day is . . .

1. He took a swim in the swamp and accidentally got clean.

Knock, Knock! GO AWAY!

Knock, knock.

Who's there?

Ogre!

Ogre who?

O-gre take a flying leap!

Knock, knock.

Who's there?

Ogre!

Ogre who?

**Ogre my dead body will
I let you in!**

Knock, knock.

Who's there?

Donkey!

Donkey who?

Donk-ey know I don't want any visitors?

Knock, knock.

Who's there?

Dragon

Dragon who?

Dragon out of here . . .

you're going too slow!

Knock, knock.

Who's there?

Puss!

Puss who?

Puss the gate shut

on your way out!

FIONA'S FAVOURITE FUNNIES!

Favourite Place? Shrekoslovakia!

Favourite Singer? Britney Spew

Why did Princess Fiona buy a shovel shop?

She wanted to be the Queen of Spades!

Why did Princess Fiona go to medical school?

She wanted to be the Queen of Hearts!

Why did Princess Fiona go out dancing every night?

She wanted to be the Queen of Clubs!

Why did Princess Fiona go to the jewellery shop?

To be the Queen of Diamonds, of course!

Through an Ogre's Eyes: How to Stay Beautiful

Hair: Be sure to wash your hair as seldom as possible. Don't risk running out of oil for the bugs and other critters in there.

Skin: Bathe regularly in water that is (at least) as thick as a hearty pea soup.

Teeth: Brush only after you have run out of all possible storage space between your molars.

Fingernails: Keep them long, but beware too sharp a point on the end. Otherwise nose-picking can be hazardous to your health.

Toenails: Don't overindulge. Allow several weeks between harvesting. The longer the jam sits there, the better if will be.

Figure: Don't sweat the big stuff. Consider this:
Once I was a beauty and all I did was preen,
Getting ready for my prince on the day
I would be queen.
Then I met an ogre, the most handsome thing I'd seen
And now I couldn't be happier that
I'm plump and really green.

Disclaimer: Fiona prefers to shower more often, but sometimes she goes gross to keep her ogre happy.

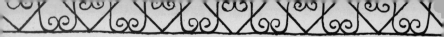

OGRESS HUMOUR

Why did Fiona leave the kingdom of Far Far Away and move to the swamp?

She wanted to live in the shrub-urbs!

How does Fiona keep all her books so well organized?

She's an alphabetical ogre!

What do you get when you cross an ogre with a basketball player?

Shrekille O'Neal!

What do Shrek and Fiona like to do after dinner?

Go out for an evening troll.

What's brown and slimy and squirms when you poke it?

Shrek's dinner!

Rap It UP!

I'm poppin' like balloons, I'm rockin' like a chair,

I got so much bling they call me the mule-ionnaire!

I'm the slammin' MC from the cool swamp scene,

And I got mad rhymes like Shrek's got green!

He's big as a house,

he's mean as a snake,

When it comes to farts and

bogeys, yo, Shrek really takes

the cake!

He's a nasty swamp monster, but

I love him to the end,

'Cause that stinky

slimy ogre is my very

best friend!

Shrek went out to gather firewood. While he was in the forest, he saw Donkey standing in the middle of the swamp, shouting for no reason.

Shrek didn't say anything to Donkey. But the next day, he saw Donkey yelling and shouting in the empty swamp again. And again the next day. Finally, on the fourth day, when Shrek saw Donkey yelling and screaming again, he decided he'd better say something.

"Hey, Donkey," Shrek called. "What are you yelling at?"

Donkey looked at Shrek and said, "Fiona told me if I shouted enough, I'd become a **little horse!**"

A DONKEY'S IDEA OF FUN

What do you call a three-legged donkey?

A wonkey!

Why did the donkey stand outside in the blizzard?

He wanted to be a cool mule!

How do you make a dragonfly?

Take away her skateboard!

What do you call a donkey who does all his chores?

A thorough burro!

Puss's Vocabulary Lesson #1

To be very, very angry	Fur-ious
A luxury automobile	Cat-illac
An ideal situation	Purr-fect
A golfer's assistant	Cat-tie
A slight delay	A paws
Product to improve garden	Fur-tilizer

Knock, knock.

Who's there?

Cattle.

Cattle who?

**This cattle drive
you crazy!**

Gotta Fur Ball? Don't Throw It Away!

Puss's Top Ten Ways To Use Those Old Fur Balls:

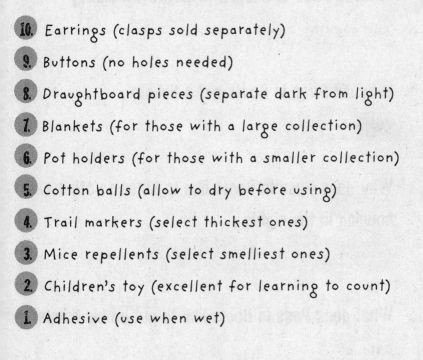

10. Earrings (clasps sold separately)

9. Buttons (no holes needed)

8. Draughtboard pieces (separate dark from light)

7. Blankets (for those with a large collection)

6. Pot holders (for those with a smaller collection)

5. Cotton balls (allow to dry before using)

4. Trail markers (select thickest ones)

3. Mice repellents (select smelliest ones)

2. Children's toy (excellent for learning to count)

1. Adhesive (use when wet)

PUSS IN BOOTS'S SCHOOL OF COMEDY

What kind of parties does Puss In Boots throw?

Hair balls!

What is Puss In Boots's favourite TV show?

The evening mews!

Why did Puss In Boots get a ticket?

For kitty littering!

Why does Puss In Boots like to listen to other cats howling in the night?

Because it's meow-sic to his ears!

What does Puss In Boots like to put on his hamburger

Catsup!

Why does Puss In Boots always win at video games?

He gets nine lives!

What do you call Puss In Boots in love?

A smitten kitten!

What would Puss In Boots call the kingdom if he were allowed to rename it?

The kingdom of Fur Fur Away!

What does Puss In Boots grow in his garden?

Catkins and pussy willows!

What does Puss In Boots do when his computer crashes?

He re-boots it!

You know why I like fairy tales?

I love a good yarn!

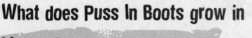

What happened when the Wicked Witch fell into the v̶ of candle wax?

She turned into a wicked wick.

Why did the wizard get confused when his wife gave birth to twins?

He couldn't tell which witch was witch.

Why did the witch give up telling fortunes?

There was no future in it.

Why wouldn't the witch go on vacation?

She was afraid she'd get broom sick.

JACK'S PRUNING AND LANDSCAPING
BEANSTALK LANE
FAR FAR UP 99999

No vegetable too tall...

Which vegetable helped me find my missing golden egg?

A potato. It was good at keeping its eyes peeled.

What do you call a really tall, green person who lives on a stalk?

A human bean!

Did you hear about my garden this year?

It was the stalk of the town!

RAPUNZEL'S
HAIR SALON
AND DAY SPA
YOU LET DOWN YOUR HAIR
AND WE'LL CUT IT!

What do you call a princess with a Mohawk?

Ra-punk-zel!

Why did Rapunzel tell her pet rabbit to stretch?

She likes long hare!

What did the farmer say when the rabbits ate all his carrots?

I'm having a bad hare day!

Where does Rapunzel like to shop?

On the mane road.

Did you hear about the princess who has hair that's fifteen feet long?

I don't know if it's true — it's just hair-say.

Where should Rapunzel go to college?

Hairvard!

Why was the man arrested for stepping on Rapunzel's hair?

Because he was tress-passing!

Once upon a time, Little Red Riding Hood was skipping through the forest when she saw the Big Bad Wolf crouched down behind a log.

"My, what big eyes you have, Mr Wolf," she said.

The wolf looked shocked. He jumped up and ran away.

A little further into the woods, Red saw the wolf again. This time he was crouched behind a tree stump.

"My, what big ears you have, Mr Wolf," she said.

Once again, the wolf couldn't have looked more surprised. He jumped up and ran away.

In the middle of the forest, Little Red Riding Hood saw the wolf yet again. This time he was crouched down behind a pile of old rocks.

"My, what big teeth you have, Mr Wolf," she said. And that's when the Big Bad Wolf jumped up and stamped his feet.

"Will you get lost?" he screamed. "I'm trying to use the bathroom!"

What would you call Little Red Riding Hood if . . .

. . . she was related to Pinocchio?

Little Red Riding Wood.

. . . her hat kept falling off?

Little Red Sliding Hood.

. . . she stopped talking?

Little Said Riding Hood.

. . . she wouldn't stop telling jokes?

Riddle Red Riding Hood.

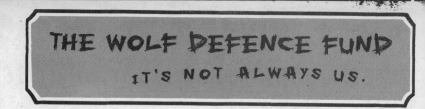

Big Bad Wolf: What do you get when you cross the Three Little Pigs with the Three Blind Mice?

Little Red Riding Hood: I don't know.

Big Bad Wolf: I don't know, either, but I'd sure like to meet 'em!

What's the first thing the wolf ate after he had his teeth cleaned?

The dentist!

WOLF!

Once upon a time, there was a farm surrounded by hills. A little boy lived there — it was his job to mind the animals. If he saw a wolf, he'd cry "wolf" to warn the townsmen of the danger.

In the hills around the farm lived a lonely wolf. Every night, the wolf would howl for hours and hours at the moon.

One day, the little boy got bored. He cried "wolf" one too many times, and his neighbours didn't come to help him when he really did need help. So he ended up being eaten by the wolf. The farm was closed and the animals moved elsewhere.

Suddenly, the night was silent. The wolf stopped howling at the moon.

One night, a bear happened upon the wolf.

"Aren't you the wolf who used to howl all night at the moon?" he asked.

The wolf nodded.

"Well, tell me," the bear said, "why don't you bay at the moon any more?"

The wolf shrugged and then replied, "No farm, no howl."

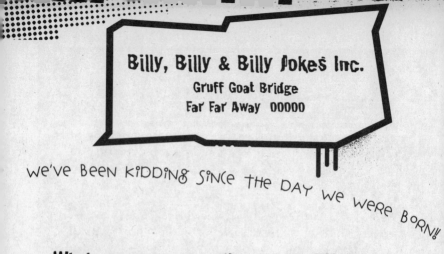

Billy, Billy & Billy Jokes Inc.
Gruff Goat Bridge
Far Far Away 00000

we've been kidding since the day we were born!!

What was mummy goat's favourite TV show?

The Nanny.

How many billy goats does it take to change a light bulb?

None. They get their kids to do it!

What do you call our facial hair?

Goatees!

Who's our favourite painter?

Vincent van Goat!

Feeling Grumpy? Bashful? Sleepy? Dopey? We can help.

What do you get when you invite Sleeping Beauty and Snow White to your house?

A slumber party that lasts a hundred years!

Why was Snow White chosen to be a judge?

Because she was the fairest in the land.

If Dwarves Had Superpowers . . .

DWARF   SPECIAL POWER

Sleepy   Can seal sleepy eyes together with eye crust in thirty seconds flat.

Dopey   Becomes dumber than a slug in a flash.

Grumpy   Insta-snap allows him to yell at people before they do anything.

Happy   Capable of happiness in any situation. Can smile while eating fish eyes and other ogre favourites.

Doc   Can turn a tissue into a dripping, slimy skin moistener with the snap of a finger . . . or the sneeze of a nose.

Bashful   Supersonic shyness can actually make him disappear.

Sneezy   High-powered snot expressor allows sneezes to blanket entire region.

Bargains! Bargains! Bargains!

Our prices are so low, you'll almost think you're stealing!

How does Robin Hood send messages in the forest?

By moss code.

Who brings a basket of food to her grandmother and then steals her jewellery?

Little Red Robin Hood.

How do sheep keep warm in the winter?

Central bleating.

What do you call a sheep on a trampoline?

A woolly jumper!

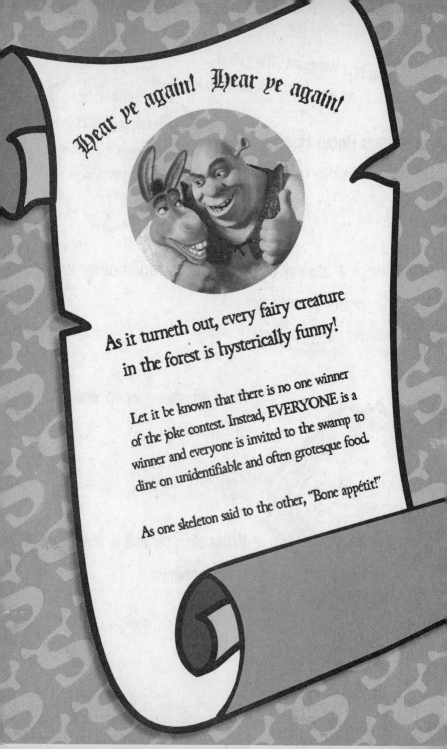

As it turneth out, every fairy creature in the forest is hysterically funny!

Let it be known that there is no one winner of the joke contest. Instead, EVERYONE is a winner and everyone is invited to the swamp to dine on unidentifiable and often grotesque food.

As one skeleton said to the other, "Bone appétit!"